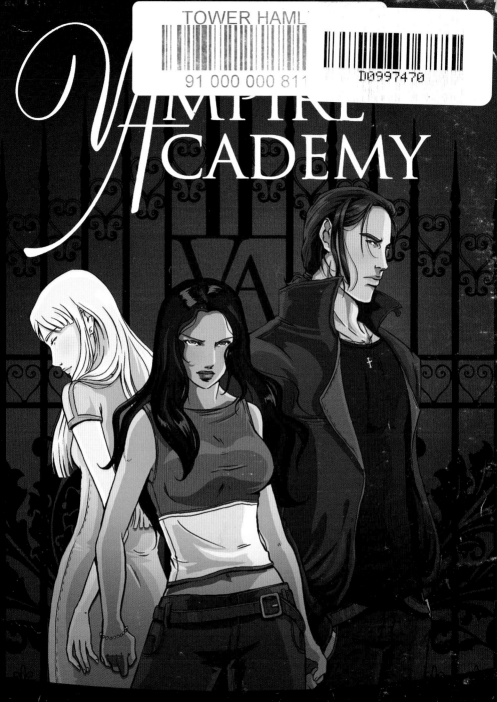

Vampire Academy

BASED ON THE #1 INTERNATIONAL BESTSELLING SERIES BY

RICHELLE MEAD

ADAPTED BY LEIGH DRAGOON • ILLUSTRATED BY EMMA VIECELI
COLOURED BY VICKI PANGESTU, FANDY, SOULCORE, JULIA, VINO OF CARAVAN STUDIO
COVER DESIGN AND LETTERING BY CHING N. CHAN

razor
bill

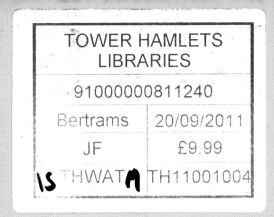
RAZORBILL

Published by the Penguin Group
Penguin Books Ltd, 80 Strand, London WC2R 0RL, England
Penguin Group (USA) Inc., 375 Hudson Street, New York, New York 10014, USA
Penguin Group (Canada), 90 Eglinton Avenue East, Suite 700, Toronto, Ontario, Canada M4P 2Y3
(a division of Pearson Penguin Canada Inc.)
Penguin Ireland, 25 St Stephen's Green, Dublin 2, Ireland (a division of Penguin Books Ltd)
Penguin Group (Australia), 250 Camberwell Road, Camberwell, Victoria 3124, Australia
(a division of Pearson Australia Group Pty Ltd)
Penguin Books India Pvt Ltd, 11 Community Centre, Panchsheel Park, New Delhi – 110 017, India
Penguin Group (NZ), 67 Apollo Drive, Rosedale, Auckland 0632, New Zealand
(a division of Pearson New Zealand Ltd)
Penguin Books (South Africa) (Pty) Ltd, 24 Sturdee Avenue, Rosebank, Johannesburg 2196, South Africa

Penguin Books Ltd, Registered Offices: 80 Strand, London WC2R 0RL, England

penguin.com

Published simultaneously in the USA and Great Britain in Razorbill,
an imprint of Penguin Books Ltd, 2011
001 – 10 9 8 7 6 5 4 3 2 1

Printed by Graphicom, Italy

British Library Cataloguing in Publication Data
A CIP catalogue record for this book is available from the British Library

ISBN: 978–0–141–33860–6

UHHH . . . I HAD THAT DREAM.

I KNOW.

WHEN DID WE LAST DO A FEEDING? WHY DIDN'T YOU SAY ANYTHING?

YOU WERE BUSY. I DIDN'T WANT TO—

HURRRRR

THE CAT LIKES LISSA BECAUSE SHE'S A MOROI. ANIMALS DON'T LIKE DHAMPIRS LIKE ME.

COME ON, LET'S DO THIS. IT'LL MAKE YOU FEEL BETTER.

MY HEART RACES WITH FEAR AND ANTICIPATION.

GASP!

SHE LOOKS MORE LIKE AN ANGEL THAN A VAMPIRE.

FEEDING IS BETTER THAN SEX—OR SO I IMAGINE SINCE I'VE NEVER HAD SEX.

SUDDENLY IT'S OVER AND I'M THRUST BACK INTO THE REAL WORLD.

YOU OKAY?

I'M GOING TO GET YOU SOMETHING TO EAT.

I...YEAH. I JUST NEED TO SLEEP IT OFF.

RRRRAAAAAWWRRRRRRRRRRRR

THE CAT SENSES SOMETHING. SOMETHING THAT'S PUT HIM ON EDGE.

THE SAME THING THAT HE SENSES IN ME: A DHAMPIR.

GASP!

LISS, WE HAVE TO GO. NOW.

LISSA'S *FEAR* POURS INTO ME THROUGH OUR PSYCHIC BOND.

WHAT'S WRONG?

GET HIS CAR KEYS.

JEREMY, LOOK AT ME.

WE NEED TO BORROW YOUR CAR. WHERE ARE YOUR KEYS?

LISSA HAS THE ABILITY TO CONTROL HUMANS.

LISSA AND I HAVE BEEN BEST FRIENDS EVER SINCE KINDERGARTEN.

THEY WON'T. I WON'T LET THEM.

ROSE!

ROSE, WHAT ARE WE GOING TO DO IF THEY CATCH US?

I HOPE I'M WORTHY OF THAT KIND OF TRUST.

SORRY... STILL WOOZY... FROM THE BLOOD LOSS...

DO YOU HEAR THAT?

BUT SHE HAS COMPLETE FAITH THAT I WILL TAKE CARE OF EVERYTHING.

HUFF HUFF HUFF...

RUN!

ST. VLADIMIR'S ACADEMY.
HOME SWEET HOME.

I'VE SPENT A LOT OF TIME IN THIS OFFICE.

HEADMISTRESS KIROVA.

MISS DRAGOMIR, YOU COULD HAVE BEEN THE ONE TO ORCHESTRATE THE ENTIRE PLAN.

BUT IT WAS STILL MISS HATHAWAY'S DUTY TO ENSURE YOU DID NOT CARRY IT OUT.

ROSE DIDN'T KIDNAP ME. I WENT WITH HER OF MY OWN FREE WILL. I DON'T WANT YOU TO BLAME HER.

I DID MY DUTY! I PROTECTED LISSA! I KEPT HER SAFE WHEN *NONE* OF *YOU* COULD!

MISS HATHAWAY, FORGIVE ME IF I FAIL TO SEE HOW TAKING VASILISA OUT OF A HEAVILY GUARDED, MAGICALLY SECURED ENVIRONMENT IS PROTECTING HER.

AS A MOROI, THE PRINCESS MUST CONTINUE ON HERE AT THE ACADEMY FOR HER OWN SAFETY—BUT WE HAVE NO SUCH OBLIGATIONS TO YOU.

NO! ROSE *HAS* TO STAY! SHE'S GOING TO BE MY GUARDIAN!

I KNOW WHAT YOUR PARENTS WANTED, GOD REST THEIR SOULS, BUT MISS HATHAWAY HAS PROVEN THAT SHE DOESN'T DESERVE TO BE A GUARDIAN.

WHAT? YOU WANT TO SEND ME AWAY? WHERE? TO MY MOM IN NEPAL? DID SHE EVEN KNOW I WAS GONE?

MISS HATHAWAY. YOU ARE OUT OF LINE.

MS. KIROVA, IF I MAY...

THEY HAVE A BOND. ROSE KNOWS WHAT VASILISA IS THINKING.

NO... THAT'S IMPOSSIBLE. THAT HASN'T HAPPENED IN CENTURIES.

THE BEST GUARDIANS ALWAYS HAD THAT BOND.

IN THE STORIES.

STORIES THAT ARE CENTURIES OLD. SURELY YOU AREN'T SUGGESTING WE LET HER STAY.

SHE MIGHT BE WILD AND DISRESPECTFUL—

WILD AND DISRESPECTFUL? WHO THE HELL ARE YOU, ANYWAY?

GUARDIAN BELIKOV IS THE PRINCESS'S GUARDIAN NOW.

YOU GOT CHEAP FOREIGN LABOR TO PROTECT LISSA?

YOU SEE? COMPLETELY UNDISCIPLINED.

SO TEACH HER DISCIPLINE. CLASSES JUST STARTED. PUT HER BACK IN AND GET HER TRAINING AGAIN.

EVEN IF WE PUT HER BACK IN TRAINING SESSIONS,

SHE COULDN'T POSSIBLY PASS HER TRIALS IN THE SPRING.

SHE'S TWO YEARS BEHIND THE OTHER NOVICES!

I'M WILLING TO MENTOR ROSE. I'LL GIVE HER EXTRA SESSIONS ALONG WITH HER NORMAL ONES.

PLEASE, MS. KIROVA. LET ROSE STAY.

OH, LISSA . . . BE CAREFUL.

SHE HAS ONLY TRIED OUT HER COMPULSION ABILITY ON HUMANS SO FAR. . . .

USING IT ON A MOROI LIKE KIROVA IS, WELL . . . **RISKY.**

FINE. MISS HATHAWAY MAY STAY AT ST. VLADIMIR'S . . . *ON A PROBATIONARY BASIS.*

YOU ARE BEING OFFERED A VERY GENEROUS DEAL. I SUGGEST YOU DON'T LET YOUR ATTITUDE ENDANGER IT.

GENEROUS, MY ASS.

FINE. I ACCEPT.

GOOD. THE QUEEN IS SCHEDULED TO VISIT THE ACADEMY SOON, AND I WANT YOU BOTH ON YOUR BEST BEHAVIOR.

UNCLE VICTOR!

VICTOR DASHKOV: A DEAR FRIEND OF LISSA'S FATHER.

I AM SO GLAD YOU'RE SAFE!

HE LOOKS SO DIFFERENT.

YES. PRINCE DASHKOV'S DISEASE IS TAKING ITS TOLL.

IT'S NOT FAIR. HE SHOULD HAVE BEEN KING. IF HE HADN'T GOTTEN SICK—

ILLNESS AND DEATH ARE RARELY FAIR.

NOW GO GET CHANGED. YOU'RE ALREADY LATE FOR TRAINING.

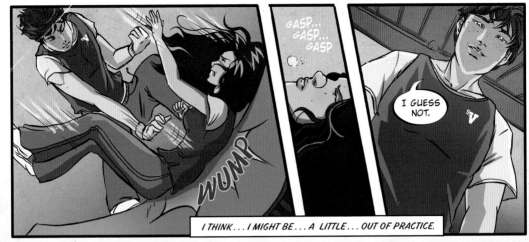

GASP...
GASP...
GASP

I GUESS NOT.

I THINK.... I MIGHT BE... A LITTLE... OUT OF PRACTICE.

I THINK I HATE YOU, MASON.

YOU'D HATE ME MORE IF I HELD BACK.

Bodyguard Theory & Personal Protection 3

Instr. Stan Alto

GET CLEANED UP AND I'LL WALK WITH YOU TO ALTO'S CLASS.

NOW, MISS HATHAWAY, YOU MUST HAVE HAD *SOME* SORT OF PLAN WHEN YOU DECIDED TO TAKE AN UNDERAGE MOROI ROYAL OUT OF THE ACADEMY AND EXPOSE HER TO CONSTANT STRIGOI THREAT.

I SHOULD JUST TELL HIM TO FUCK OFF...

WE NEVER RAN INTO ANY STRIGOI.

OBVIOUSLY, SEEING AS HOW YOU'RE STILL ALIVE. AND THE *ONLY* REASON THAT YOU TWO ARE ALIVE IS THAT YOU GOT *LUCKY*.

YOU'RE EXAGGERATING! STRIGOI AREN'T LURKING AROUND EVERY CORNER OUT THERE! IT'S SAFER THAN YOU MAKE IT SOUND.

SAFER? WE ARE AT WAR WITH THE STRIGOI! YOU MAY HAVE MORE SPEED AND STRENGTH THAN A MOROI OR A HUMAN, BUT A DHAMPIR IS *NOTHING* COMPARED TO A STRIGOI.

NO WAY AM I GONNA LET THIS JERK MAKE ME CRY.

NOW TELL ME, WHAT IS IT THAT MAKES THEM SO POWERFUL?

MOROI BLOOD.

I'M SORRY? WHAT WAS THAT? I CAN'T QUITE HEAR YOU.

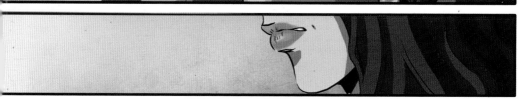

MOROI BLOOD! MOROI BLOOD MAKES THEM STRONGER!

YES, AND FOR THAT REASON THEY HUNGER FOR MOROI BLOOD OVER ALL ELSE. EVEN WE GUARDIANS CAN'T PROTECT ALL THE MOROI IN OUR CHARGE.

SOME MOROI BELIEVE THE SITUATION IS SO HOPELESS THEY TURN STRIGOI BY CHOICE.

Moroi:
Mortal vampires. Need to drink blood to survive, can use elemental magic. Alive. Born.

Strigoi:
Former Moroi, dhampirs, or even humans. They lose their ability to use elemental magic when they turn. Moroi blood makes them immortal and grants them extra power and speed. Undead. Immortal. Made as opposed to born.

Dhampir:
half Moroi, half human.

AND AS THE MOROI DISAPPEAR, SO, TOO, DO DHAMPIRS LIKE OURSELVES.

BECAUSE, AS YOU KNOW, DHAMPIRS REQUIRE MOROI PARTNERS TO REPRODUCE.

FINALLY . . . I EARNED MY LUNCH ESCAPE.

IT LOOKS TO *ME* LIKE EVERYTHING YOU'RE WEARING CAME FROM A *GARAGE SALE.* I THOUGHT DRAGOMIRS HAD *STANDARDS.*

OKAY, YOU'RE DONE HERE.

DON'T YOU EVER TOUCH ME AGAIN!

TIMES LIKE THIS, IT'S GOOD TO HAVE A DANGEROUS REPUTATION.

GET GOING. *NOW.*

THE ELEMENTARY SCHOOL'S OVER ON THE WEST CAMPUS.

WHO THE HELL WAS THAT?

I DON'T KNOW. I WAS ON MY WAY TO THE FEEDING ROOM AND SHE RAILROADED ME. I THINK SHE'S DATING AARON.

AARON, YOUR OLD BOYFRIEND, AARON?

THE AARON YOU USED TO LOOOOVE, AARON?

THE AARON YOU *DID* *IT* WITH, AARON?

SHUT UP, ROSE!

LISSA!

NATALIE IS VICTOR DASHKOV'S DAUGHTER.

SHE'S NICE, BUT ONE OF THE MOST BORING PEOPLE I KNOW.

I KNEW YOU'D BE BACK! CAMILLE SAID ONE OF YOU GOT PREGNANT AND YOU TOOK OFF TO GET AN ABORTION. BUT I KNEW THAT COULDN'T BE TRUE.

OUR ROOM'S BEEN SO LONELY WITHOUT YOU! WHAT WAS IT LIKE BEING ON YOUR OWN? WHAT DID YOU DO FOR BLOOD?

THE LIE COMES EASILY TO MY LIPS.

OH, THAT WAS EASY. THERE ARE LOTS OF HUMANS WHO WERE WILLING TO LET HER FEED ON THEM.

IT'S NOT LIKE SHE KNOWS ANY BETTER.

REALLY?

YUP. AT PARTIES AND STUFF.

MOST OF THEM ARE SO WASTED THEY DON'T REMEMBER ANYTHING THE NEXT DAY.

FOR A DHAMPIR TO LET A MOROI TAKE BLOOD FROM THEM IS ALMOST, WELL, DIRTY.

ANYWAY, SPEAKING OF, LISSA'S HUNGRY AND WE WERE JUST ON OUR WAY TO THE FEEDERS.

CATCH YOU LATER?

PRACTICALLY PORNOGRAPHIC.

OH SURE!

I WISH I COULD THINK ON MY FEET THE WAY YOU DO.

I HAD TO THINK OF **SOMETHING**. YOU KNOW WHAT PEOPLE WOULD SAY IF THEY FOUND OUT . . .

ABOUT ME . . . DOING THAT FOR YOU.

RIGHT THIS WAY.

DAILY FEEDINGS ARE A PART OF MOROI LIFE.

WELCOME BACK, PRINCESS.

A FUNNY FEELING SETTLES OVER ME.

I GUESS I'VE GOTTEN USED TO BEING LISSA'S PRIMARY BLOOD SOURCE.

MMMMM...

DISGUST POURS INTO ME. WHAT'S WRONG WITH ME?

WHY DO I MISS IT? I'M NOT ADDICTED— NOT LIKE THIS. AND I DON'T WANT TO BE.

I NEED TO GET OUT OF HERE.

ROSE, YOU'RE LATE FOR PRACTICE.

WHATEVER YOU SAY, COMRADE.

I FEEL THE PULL JUST BEFORE IT HAPPENS.

HER EMOTIONS SO STRONG, THEY SUCK ME IN.

AND THERE I AM, SEEING THE WORLD THROUGH LISSA'S EYES.

YOU CAN HAVE THE ACADEMY, BUT NOT THE WINDOW SEAT.

DON'T WORRY, I WON'T BITE. WELL, AT LEAST NOT IN THE WAY YOU'RE AFRAID OF.

CHRISTIAN OZERA.

WHAT ARE YOU DOING HERE?

TAKING IN THE SIGHTS, OF COURSE.

WHATEVER.

HEY, WAIT A MINUTE.

. . . AND KILLED THEM.

OBVIOUSLY HE'S NOT STRIGOI HIMSELF.

LOOK, TAKE THE WINDOW SEAT. YOU CAN HAVE IT FOR TODAY.

BUT SOME PEOPLE THINK HE'S NOT FAR OFF.

ARE YOU . . . ARE YOU SURE?

YEAH, YEAH.

DON'T WORRY ABOUT IT. JUST STOP GIVING ME THOSE PUPPY-DOG EYES.

ROSE?

THE VISION FADES . . .

ARE YOU ALL RIGHT?

I . . . YEAH.

I WAS WITH . . . LISSA. THROUGH THE BOND. I WAS IN HER HEAD.

I WALKED HERE . . .

I CHANGED MY CLOTHES . . .

I DID ALL THAT WHILE I WAS IN LISSA'S HEAD.

IS SHE ALL RIGHT?

YEAH... SHE'S... SHE'S NOT IN DANGER.

UMM... SO... HOW DID YOU END UP AT THE ACADEMY? YOU WEREN'T EVEN HERE A FEW YEARS AGO.

I USED TO BE GUARDIAN FOR A ZEKLOS LORD. HE WAS KILLED RECENTLY. NOT ON MY WATCH... NOT THAT IT MAKES IT ANY BETTER.

I'D BLAME MYSELF, TOO, IF SOMETHING HAPPENED TO LISSA.

SO... UM... DID YOU COME UP WITH THE PLAN TO GET US BACK? BECAUSE THAT WHOLE THING WAS PRETTY GOOD.

CAN'T GO WRONG WITH BRUTE FORCE AND ALL.

BOW

THIS MAN IS ALMOST TOO GOOD-LOOKING FOR HIS OWN GOOD.

I'M GLAD IT MET WITH YOUR SATISFACTION.

COME ON. I WANT TO SEE YOU DO TWENTY REPS ON THIS MACHINE.

HAVEN'T I DONE ENOUGH TODAY?

NOT IF YOU WANT TO PASS YOUR TRIALS AND END UP ASSIGNED TO SOMEONE IN THE SPRING.

I WANT TO BE ASSIGNED TO LISSA. NO ONE ELSE.

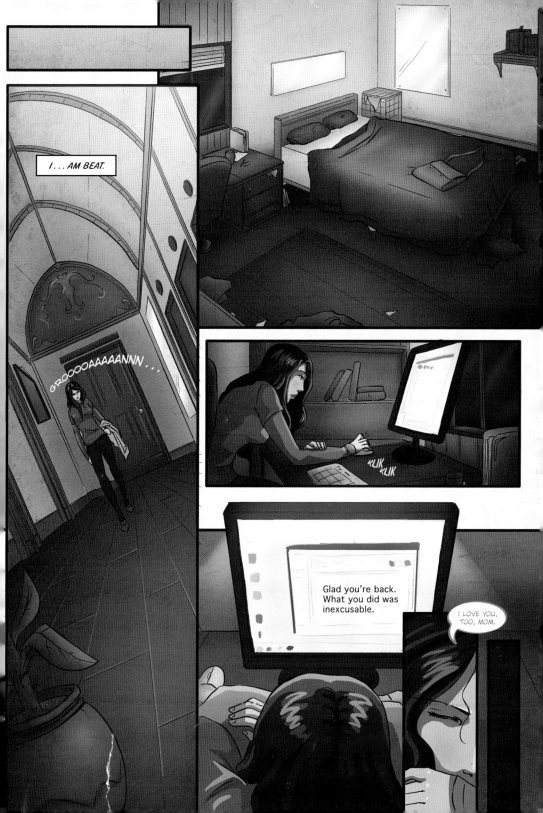

YOU WERE IN MY HEAD AGAIN? FOR *THAT* LONG?

I DIDN'T DO IT ON PURPOSE. IT JUST HAPPENED. AND THAT'S NOT THE POINT. HOW LONG DID YOU HANG OUT WITH HIM AFTERWARD?

I CAN'T BELIEVE SHE LET HIM KNOW ABOUT OUR BLOOD ARRANGEMENT.

NOT THAT LONG.

IF THAT GETS OUT IT'LL KILL US BOTH SOCIALLY.

CHRISTIAN'S *DANGEROUS*, LISSA.

YOU'RE OVERREACTING. HE'S NOT GOING TO TURN STRIGOI.

HE'S A BAD INFLUENCE.

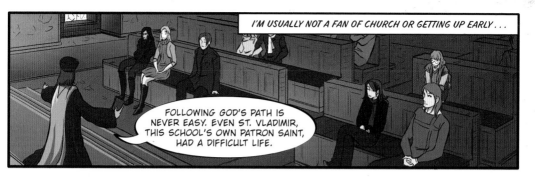

I'M USUALLY NOT A FAN OF CHURCH OR GETTING UP EARLY...

FOLLOWING GOD'S PATH IS NEVER EASY. EVEN ST. VLADIMIR, THIS SCHOOL'S OWN PATRON SAINT, HAD A DIFFICULT LIFE.

HE COULD HEAL THE SICK...

...BUT AT LEAST IT GIVES ME A CHANCE TO HANG OUT WITH LISSA.

THE PRIEST'S WORDS TRAILED OFF. UNTIL...

...AND SO IT WAS WITH HIS GUARDIAN, SHADOW-KISSED ANNA.

SHADOW-KISSED. THOSE WORDS BURNED INTO ME.

HELLO, ROSE. IT'S NICE TO SEE YOU AGAIN.

I HOPE HE DOESN'T THINK I'M INTERESTED IN VOLUNTEER WORK.

YEAH, YOU, TOO.

UM... I HEARD YOU TALK ABOUT ANNA. ABOUT HER BEING "SHADOW-KISSED." WHAT DOES THAT MEAN?

I'M NOT ENTIRELY SURE. IT MIGHT HAVE JUST BEEN A NAME OR TITLE SHE WAS GIVEN TO MAKE HER SOUND FIERCE.

OH. SO... WHO WAS SHE?

I MENTIONED IT A NUMBER OF TIMES.

MOROI SAINTS

OH. I... UM... MUST HAVE MISSED IT.

YOU CAN LEARN ABOUT HER IN HERE.

GREAT. HOMEWORK.

UM... THANKS.

HEY, HANDS OFF THE MERCHANDISE.

I WAS JUST TELLING PAUL ABOUT THE TROUBLE YOU USED TO CAUSE IN MS. KARP'S CLASS.

BEFORE HER FREAK-OUT, THAT IS.

JESSE ZEKLOS.

MAN, SHE WAS MESSED UP. USED TO THINK PEOPLE WERE AFTER HER, AND SHE'D ALWAYS GO OFF ON STUFF THAT DIDN'T MAKE ANY SENSE.

SHE USED TO WANDER CAMPUS WHILE EVERYONE WAS ASLEEP.

I'D RUN INTO MS. KARP ONE NIGHT AS I TRIED TO SNEAK OUT OF MY DORM ROOM.

YOU SHOULD BE MORE CAREFUL, ROSEMARIE.

THUD

I REMEMBER A TINGLE BURNING INTO MY SKIN.

IT WAS LIKE THE CUT WAS NEVER THERE. I'D SEEN A LOT OF MOROI MAGIC... BUT NEVER ANYTHING LIKE THAT.

WHAT'S THAT BOOK?

NOTHING. JUST A LOT OF EXTRA WORK I GOT BY OPENING MY FAT MOUTH.

AS WE STEP OUT OF THE CHURCH I SENSE THAT SOMETHING ISN'T RIGHT.

BY THE TIME I REALIZE WHAT'S HAPPENING, IT'S TOO LATE.

THAT LITTLE BITCH.

HEY, I'M GUESSING THAT WATER IS YOUR ELEMENT? WHAT A COINCIDENCE THAT A BUNCH JUST FELL ON US.

MS. KIROVA'S GOING TO HAVE SOMETHING TO SAY WHEN SHE FINDS OUT YOU USED MAGIC AGAINST OTHER STUDENTS.

LIKE I NEED TO EXPLAIN MYSELF TO A PEASANT LIKE YOU. ANYWAY, I DIDN'T DO ANYTHING. THAT WAS AN ACT OF GOD.

YOU SHOULD STEAL AARON BACK JUST TO TEACH THAT BITCH A LESSON.

HER NAME IS MIA, APPARENTLY. AND I'M OVER AARON.

I DON'T WANT TO TEACH ANYONE A LESSON.

I HAVE TO DO SOMETHING ABOUT THIS MIA GIRL.

COME ON. YOU'RE SOAKED. TAKE MY COAT.

HERE. IT'S WATERPROOF. I'VE GOT ANOTHER TRAINING SESSION NEXT. I'LL WORK UP A SWEAT IN NO TIME.

GO ON AND CHANGE! I'LL SEE YOU IN CLASS!

HEY, MASON.

I SAW WHAT HAPPENED. SO WHEN'S THE BIG CATFIGHT GOING TO HAPPEN?

I'M SURE I DON'T KNOW WHAT YOU MEAN.

DO YOU KNOW ANYTHING ABOUT MIA? WHY'S SHE GUNNING FOR LISSA?

I'M NOT SURE. SHE SHOULDN'T BE PUTTING ON AIRS, THOUGH. HER PARENTS ARE PRACTICALLY SERVANTS.

REALLY?

WHAT I LOVE ABOUT MASON IS THAT HE THINKS JUST LIKE I DO.

YEP. HER DAD CUTS GRASS AND HER MOM'S A MAID. THEY WORK FOR A MOROI ROYAL.

AND NO ONE KNOWS?

NO ONE. AND I DEFINITELY GET THE FEELING SHE'D LIKE TO KEEP IT THAT WAY. YOU KNOW HOW THE ROYALS ARE.

I ACTUALLY HAVE A LOT OF RESPECT FOR ANYONE WHO PULLS A FULL DAY'S WORK.

WELL, EXCEPT FOR LISSA.

BUT IT'S ANOTHER MATTER ENTIRELY WHEN SOMEONE'S TRYING TO PASS HERSELF OFF AS SOMETHING SHE'S NOT.

And with Vladimir always is Anna, the daughter of Fyodor. Their love is as chaste and pure as that of brother and sister, and many times has she defended him from Strigoi who would seek to destroy him and his holiness. Likewise, it is she who comforts him when the spirit becomes too much to bear, and Satan's darkness tries to smother him and weaken his own health and body. This, too, she defends against, for they have been bound together ever since he saved her life as a child. It is a sign of God's love that He has sent the blessed Vladimir a guardian such as her, one who is shadow-kissed and always knows what is in her heart and mind.

BUT WHAT DOES IT MEAN TO BE SHADOW-KISSED?

OKAY. I'LL CUT HIS HEAD OFF.

IGNORING THE FACT THAT YOU DON'T HAVE A WEAPON AND THAT HE MAY BE A FOOT TALLER THAN YOU.

FINE. THEN I SET HIM ON FIRE.

AGAIN, WITH WHAT?

AAHHHH!

THWAP

THIS GUY'S A JERK. I GIVE UP.

SO, COMRADE, WHAT DO I DO?

YOU RUN.

*DOES HE THINK I'M **PRETTY**?*

IT HAPPENED TO MY MOM. SHE USED TO BE BEAUTIFUL. I GUESS SHE STILL IS, SORT OF. I HAVEN'T SEEN HER IN A WHILE.

YOU DON'T LIKE YOUR MOTHER?

SHE ABANDONED ME. SHE LEFT ME TO BE RAISED BY THE ACADEMY.

THEN IT HAPPENS. TERROR EXPLODES FROM MY BODY AND IN MY HEAD.

GASP!

WHAT'S WRONG? WHAT HAPPENED?

IT...IT WAS STILL ALIVE WHEN I GOT BACK.

POOR THING. IT MUST HAVE SUFFERED SO MUCH...

I CAN FEEL EVERYONE'S EYES ON US.

DON'T!

LADIES.

MS. KARP?!

YOU THINK I WOULDN'T NOTICE YOU SKIPPING CLASS? MUST BE THE NICE WEATHER.

WOOOSH

WHAT IS IT? IS IT A CROW?

TOO BIG. IT'S A RAVEN.

IS IT DEAD?

DEFINITELY DEAD. DON'T TOUCH IT.

LISSA HADN'T LISTENED TO ME BACK THEN . . .

COME ON, WE HAVE TO GET TO CLASS.

WOLVES, LIKE MANY OTHER SPECIES, DIFFERENTIATE THEIR PACKS INTO ALPHA MALES AND ALPHA FEMALES WHOM OTHERS DEFER TO...

WHAT ABOUT FOXES? DO *THEY* HAVE ALPHAS, TOO?

ADMIT IT: YOU KILLED THE FOX SO KIROVA WILL THINK YOU'RE CRAZY.

RALF SARCOZY.

SCREW YOU.

CHRISTIAN OZERA: FIRE USER.

MR. OZERA, HOW DARE YOU! DO YOU HAVE ANY IDEA? REPORT TO HEADMISTRESS KIROVA'S OFFICE NOW!

SURE THING, MS. MEISSNER.

HE MIGHT REALLY AND TRULY BE A PSYCHO.

EXILED IN MY DORM ROOM.

IF EVER THERE WAS A TIME FOR ME TO SLIP INTO LISSA'S MIND, IT WAS NOW.

BUT I DIDN'T KNOW HOW TO CONTROL IT.

IT TAKES A WHILE.

THEN THE WALL CAME DOWN. I'M IN.

YOU SHOULDN'T HAVE DONE THAT TO RALF.

HE WAS HASSLING YOU AND ROSE, AND IT'S NOT LIKE I HURT HIM.

I JUST SCARED HIM A LITTLE. BESIDES, THIS'LL SHUT EVERYONE UP ABOUT THE FOX.

DON'T MAKE IT SOUND LIKE YOU DID ALL THIS JUST FOR ME. ATTACKING SOMEONE WITH MAGIC IS FORBIDDEN, AND THAT'S *EXACTLY* WHY YOU WANTED TO DO IT.

YOU DON'T KNOW ANYTHING ABOUT MY PARENTS.

YOU'RE RIGHT.

I HAD NO RIGHT. I'M SORRY.

A FEELING OF PEACE SETTLES OVER HER. A FEELING I THOUGHT ONLY I COULD BRING.

THAWCK

DAMMIT!

I NEED TO FIND A DISTRACTION.

WERE YOU REALLY PLANNING ON STUDYING TONIGHT?

JESSE.

I HAD TO DO AN ASSIGNMENT WITH *MEREDITH.*

BUT YOU'RE A LOT HOTTER THAN SHE IS.

I HAVE NO INTENTION OF LOSING MY VIRGINITY ON A COUCH IN A LOUNGE.

I'M NOT HAVING SEX, OKAY?

OKAY.

WELL? YOU SEE SOMETHING YOU LIKE?

PLEASE GET DRESSED.

PEOPLE TALK, AND YOUR BEHAVIOR REFLECTS POORLY, NOT ONLY ON YOURSELF, BUT ON LISSA, TOO. AND ME.

I'M SEVENTEEN. I SHOULD BE ABLE TO ENJOY IT.

YES. YOU'RE SEVENTEEN, AND IN LESS THAN A YEAR SOMEONE'S LIFE WILL BE IN YOUR HANDS.

I MET IVAN ZEKLOS WHEN I WAS SEVENTEEN. WE WERE FRIENDS.

I WAS A TOP STUDENT, I PAID ATTENTION TO EVERYTHING IN MY CLASSES . . . AND IN THE END IT STILL WASN'T ENOUGH.

THAT'S HOW THIS LIFE IS. YOU CAN'T AFFORD FUN. ONE SLIP, ONE DISTRACTION . . .

AND IT'S TOO LATE.

THE QUEEN'S ARRIVAL. A LOT OF CEREMONY AND POSTURING.

DHAMPIRS ARE LINED UP TOWARD THE BACK.

WHILE MOROI AND REPRESENTATIVES OF THE TWELVE ROYAL FAMILIES STAND UP FRONT.

VASILISA DRAGOMIR.

IT'S A BIG DEAL TO BE ACKNOWLEDGED BY QUEEN TATIANA.

THEY WERE AMONG THE FINEST OF MOROI. DRAGOMIR KINGS AND QUEENS HAVE RULED WISELY. THE DRAGOMIR NAME COMMANDS RESPECT.

WE ARE GLAD YOU HAVE RETURNED. WE DEEPLY REGRET THE LOSS OF YOUR PARENTS AND YOUR BROTHER.

THANK YOU, YOUR MAJESTY.

BUT, AS YOU HAVE DEMONSTRATED, NAMES DO *NOT* MAKE A PERSON.

I'LL KILL THE QUEEN. SHE CAN'T GET AWAY WITH THAT.

SHE'S SCARED AND UPSET. UNSTABLE.

LISSA!

SHE SHOULDN'T HAVE SAID THAT. IT WASN'T RIGHT.

DON'T LET IT BOTHER YOU.

WELL...I SHOULD GO FIND DADDY. I'LL SEE YOU BACK IN THE ROOM.

AT LEAST THE QUEEN KNOWS HER NAME, WHICH IS MORE THAN I CAN SAY FOR YOU AND YOUR WANNABE-ROYAL ACT. *OR* YOUR PARENTS.

AT LEAST I *SEE* MY PARENTS.

AT LEAST I KNOW WHO THEY BOTH ARE. GOD ONLY KNOWS WHO YOUR FATHER IS.

AND YOUR MOM'S ONE OF THE MOST FAMOUS GUARDIANS AROUND, BUT SHE COULDN'T CARE LESS ABOUT YOU.

SHE'S BUSY PROTECTING ROYALS, NOT CLEANING UP AFTER THEM.

WHAT DID YOU SAY?

SLEEP CAME RELUCTANTLY.

LISSA. SCARED AND UPSET.

SOMETHING IS WRONG. TERRIBLY WRONG.

WHERE DO YOU THINK YOU'RE GOING?

I NEED TO SEE DIM—GUARDIAN BELIKOV.

WHAT RABBIT?

I CLEANED IT UP. SO NATALIE WOULDN'T SEE.

DID SHE TRY TO HEAL THE RABBIT?

TELL ME WHAT HAPPENED.

I CAME BACK ABOUT AN HOUR AGO. AND IT WAS THERE. RIGHT IN THE MIDDLE OF THE FLOOR. TORN APART.

MOROI MAGIC COULD CONJURE FIRE AND WATER, MOVE ROCKS... BUT NO ONE COULD HEAL OR BRING ANIMALS BACK FROM THE DEAD.

NO ONE EXCEPT MS. KARP.

I DIDN'T WANT NATALIE TO FIND IT. I DIDN'T WANT TO SCARE HER. SO I CLEANED IT UP.

THEN I JUST COULDN'T . . . I COULDN'T GO BACK.

DO YOU KNOW WHO DID IT?

I KNOW WHO YOU ARE. YOU WON'T SURVIVE BEING HERE. I'LL MAKE SURE OF IT. LEAVE NOW. IT'S THE ONLY WAY YOU MIGHT LIVE THROUGH THIS.

PEOPLE ARE TALKING ABOUT US.

I KNOW. IGNORE THEM.

EXCUSE ME?

COME ON, ROSE, I *BLEED* FOR YOU.

WAIT, IT IS ROSE WHO DOES THE BLEEDING, RIGHT?

HEHE

PSST

HEHE

THEY KNOW HOW I FED YOU WHILE WE WERE GONE.

HOW?

HOW DO YOU THINK? YOUR *FRIEND* CHRISTIAN.

NO, HE WOULDN'T HAVE.

WHO ELSE KNEW?

I'M GOING TO KILL YOU.

TELL HER SHE'S WRONG. TELL HER YOU DIDN'T SPREAD THOSE STORIES ABOUT HER.

I KNOW IT'S IMPOSSIBLE TO BELIEVE A FREAK LIKE ME COULD KEEP HIS MOUTH SHUT . . .

YOU WANT SOMEONE TO BLAME. BLAME YOUR GOLDEN BOY OVER THERE.

...BUT I HAVE BETTER THINGS TO DO THAN SPREAD STUPID RUMORS.

HEHE

JESSE DOESN'T KNOW.

HE DOES, THOUGH. DOESN'T HE, ROSE?

HE DOES KNOW. HE'D FIGURED IT OUT THAT NIGHT IN THE LOUNGE.

YOU *TOLD* HIM?

NO, HE GUESSED.

HE APPARENTLY DID MORE THAN GUESS.

WHAT'S THAT SUPPOSED TO MEAN?

OH, I GET IT. HE SAID WE HAD SEX.

AND, UH, RALF, TOO.

THAT ASSHOLE! I'M GOING TO—

HE ALSO SAID— THEY BOTH SAID—THAT YOU LET THEM . . .

WELL, YOU LET THEM DRINK YOUR BLOOD.

THAT'S CRAZY! ROSE WOULD NEVER . . .

WE DIDN'T DO ANYTHING YOU DIDN'T WANT US TO DO. AND DON'T GO LAYING A HAND ON US. KIROVA'LL KICK YOU OUT.

AND YOU'LL HAVE TO GO LIVE WITH THE OTHER BLOOD WHORES.

SO LONG, BLOOD WHORE!

I WANT TO PUNCH THEM BOTH. BUT HE'S RIGHT. KIROVA WOULD EXPEL ME IN THE BLINK OF AN EYE.

KNOCK KNOCK

ARE YOU OKAY?

IT DOESN'T MATTER IF I AM, REMEMBER? IS LISSA OKAY?

I'M SORRY. SHE DID IT TO GET BACK AT ME.

SHE?

MIA. SHE HAS IT OUT FOR ME FOR SOME REASON.

JESSE AND RALF AREN'T SMART ENOUGH TO THINK OF SOMETHING LIKE THIS ON THEIR OWN.

THERE'S ONE THING THAT MIA WANTS MORE THAN TO DESTROY YOU AND ME. SHE WANTS TO BE ACCEPTED BY THE ROYALS. AND I CAN TAKE THAT AWAY FROM HER.

HOW?

BY *TELLING* THEM.

NO. YOU CAN'T USE COMPULSION.

THE AFTERMATH OF JESSE AND RALF'S LIES WERE AS HORRIBLE AS I'D EXPECTED.

SHE *DIDN'T* DO IT WITH JESSE. EVERYONE'S OVERREACTING.

BUT IT DIDN'T WORRY ME AS MUCH AS LISSA.

YEAH, JESSE'S LYING.

SHE'S USING COMPULSION TO WIN OVER THE OTHER ROYALS.

I DON'T KNOW WHAT YOU SEE IN MIA.

I KNOW WHAT YOU'RE DOING.

WHAT ARE YOU TALKING ABOUT?

YOU KNOW. WITH ALL YOUR LITTLE FRIENDS. OR SHOULD I SAY *SLAVES*?

I HAVE TO GO.

CHRISTIAN . . . WAIT.

MAYBE YOU'RE USING COMPULSION TO MAKE ME THINK YOU'RE A TWO-FACED BITCH.

BUT I DOUBT IT.

SHE'S TAKING THIS TOO FAR.

LISSA, YOU HAVE GOT TO LAY OFF USING COMPULSION ON EVERYONE.

YOU KNOW THIS ISN'T RIGHT. ANDRE WOULDN'T APPROVE. HE WOULDN'T BE PROUD OF YOU FOR DOING THIS.

Y-YOU'RE RIGHT. I WON'T USE COMPULSION OR HEALING ANYMORE.

GOOD.

HEY, UNCLE VICTOR'S TAKING NATALIE AND ME SHOPPING IN MISSOULA THIS WEEKEND.

HE THINKS HE CAN GET KIROVA TO LET YOU COME, TOO.

I HAVE TO ADMIT, I'M KIND OF EXCITED AT THE THOUGHT OF GETTING SOME NEW CLOTHES.

ARE YOU INTERESTED?

YEAH! DEFINITELY.

ST. VLADIMIR'S SPIRIT WAS STRONG . . .

. . . AND HE WAS TRULY GIFTED BY GOD.

WHEN HE TOUCHED THEM, THE CRIPPLED WALKED AND THE BLIND COULD SEE. WHERE HE WALKED, FLOWERS BLOOMED.

SEEMS THAT MS. KARP WASN'T THE ONLY ONE WHO COULD HEAL LIKE LISSA.

AND ALL THE WHILE THE MASSES GATHERED AROUND HIM, LOVING HIM, EAGER TO FOLLOW HIS TEACHINGS AND HEAR HIM PREACH THE WORD OF GOD. . . .

I WAS ACTUALLY LOOKING FORWARD TO GOING TO THE MALL WITH LISSA. I SHOULD HAVE KNOWN THIS WOULDN'T REALLY BE A DAY OFF.

LET'S GO OVER THE GUARD GROUPINGS AGAIN.

I REALLY WANT TO SWING BY MACY'S AND SEE IF THEY HAVE THOSE SHOES AND THAT NECKLACE I WAS TELLING YOU ABOUT.

I'M FAR GUARD. WHICH MEANS . . .

THAT YOU'LL BE IN BACK, KEEPING AN EYE ON THINGS.

YOU WILL BE LISSA'S NEAR GUARD. YOU'RE FEMALE AND THE SAME AGE—YOU CAN STAND CLOSE TO HER WITHOUT ATTRACTING ATTENTION.

AND I DON'T EVER TAKE MY EYES OFF HER.

YOU'VE GOT A STAR STUDENT THERE. YOU GIVE HER A STAKE YET?

IT WOULD BE NICE IF *SOMEONE* WOULD.

I KNOW THAT EVERY GUARDIAN IN THE VAN HAD A STAKE AND A GUN CONCEALED ON HIM.

THERE'S MORE TO KILLING STRIGOI THAN JUST USING A STAKE. YOU'VE STILL GOT TO SUBDUE THEM AND BRING YOURSELF TO KILL THEM.

WHY WOULDN'T I KILL THEM?

IT'S LIKELY YOU'LL KNOW THEM. MOST STRIGOI WERE ONCE MOROI WHO CHOSE TO TURN. SOMETIMES THEY'RE MOROI OR DHAMPIRS WHO WERE TURNED BY FORCE.

COULD YOU KILL SOMEONE YOU USED TO KNOW? IF THAT MOMENT COMES AND YOU HESITATE, YOU'LL GET KILLED.

IT REMINDS ME OF MIKHAIL HUNTING SONYA.

WHO ARE MIKHAIL AND SONYA?

WHY . . . SONYA KARP. SHE CHOSE TO KILL SOMEONE AND BECOME STRIGOI.

MS. KARP?!

MIKHAIL WAS HER LOVER. HE HUNTED HER DOWN. TO KILL HER . . .

. . . BUT HE NEVER FOUND HER. . . .

PURPOSELY HUNTING DOWN SOMEONE I LOVED . . . I DON'T KNOW IF I COULD DO THAT.

SO ARE YOU WORRIED I'M GOING TO LOSE IT LIKE MS. KARP? ARE YOU WORRIED I'LL GO STRIGOI, TOO?

EVEN IF IT'S TECHNICALLY THE RIGHT THING TO DO.

NO. NO WAY. YOU'D NEVER DO THAT.

I WAS JUST KIDDING. DON'T BE SO SERIOUS.

THIS IS PERFECT. COME ON, I'M BUYING IT FOR YOU.

SHE USUALLY OFFERS TO BUY ME ANYTHING I WANT, AND I'M USUALLY HAPPY TO TAKE HER UP ON IT.

HEY, LOOK AT THIS. IT WOULD GO GREAT WITH YOUR DRESS.

WOW. THAT'S OUT OF EVEN *HER* PRICE RANGE.

CASHIER

$5,000.0

COME ON. THE DRESS IS MORE THAN ENOUGH. EVEN YOU CAN'T AFFORD THAT, AND I HATE ROSE STUFF, ANYWAY.

THE DISAPPROVING LOOK.

BACK TO PRISON.

SO I CAN'T EVER TRY ON CLOTHES AGAIN?

YAWN

WHEN YOU AREN'T ON DUTY YOU CAN. YOU CAN DO IT DURING YOUR TIME OFF.

I DON'T EVER WANT TIME OFF. I WANT TO ALWAYS TAKE CARE OF LISSA.

I CAN'T WAIT TO SEE YOU IN THAT DRESS!

YOU WILL. IF KIROVA LETS ME—

SNAP

GASP

THE WEIRD THING IS . . . MY ANKLE DOESN'T HURT AT ALL.

YOU'RE VERY LUCKY.

IT'S NOT BROKEN OR SPRAINED. YOU PROBABLY PASSED OUT FROM THE SHOCK.

YOU MUST HAVE A GUARDIAN ANGEL.

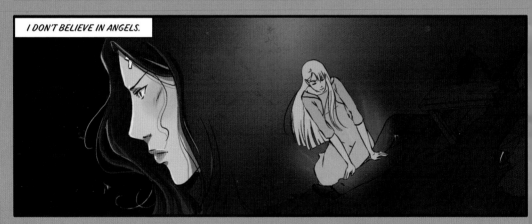

I DON'T BELIEVE IN ANGELS.

MY ANKLE DID BREAK. LISSA HEALED IT.

DID SHE HEAL ME THAT TIME, TOO?

LISSA . . . IT MAKES SENSE NOW. I SHOULDN'T HAVE SURVIVED. EVERYONE SAID SO.

I DID WHAT I HAD TO DO TO—

TO GET BACK AT MIA? I KNOW WHY SHE'S PISSED AT YOU, YOU KNOW.

WHAT ARE YOU TALKING ABOUT?

YOUR PERFECT BROTHER, ANDRE, SCREWED HER OVER— LITERALLY.

YOU'RE LYING.

I'M NOT. I USED TO TALK TO MIA BACK WHEN SHE WAS A FRESHMAN. SHE WORKED ON A COMMITTEE WITH ANDRE. THEY GOT TOGETHER.

HE TOLD HER TO KEEP QUIET ABOUT THEIR RELATIONSHIP BECAUSE HE DIDN'T WANT ANYONE TO KNOW HE WAS SEEING A NON-ROYAL.

WHEN HE GOT TIRED OF HER, HE DUMPED HER.

ANDRE WASN'T LIKE THAT! YOU DIDN'T EVEN KNOW HIM! YOU'RE LYING! GET OUT!

ANYTHING YOU WANT, YOUR HIGHNESS.

SOB

SOB

I THINK THIS IS WHAT MADNESS FEELS LIKE.

THIS ISN'T THE FIRST TIME I'VE FOUND LISSA LIKE THIS.

I'VE HELD ON TO HER SECRETS FOR SO LONG.

URGHHH . .

I BELIEVED THAT I'D BEEN HELPING HER.

YOU TOLD THEM.

I'M SORRY. I HAD TO.

I TOLD THEM ABOUT YOU CUTTING YOURSELF... AND I THINK WE NEED TO TELL THEM ABOUT THE OTHER STUFF.

ABOUT HOW YOU CAN HEAL PEOPLE. HOW YOU HEALED ME.

THEY'LL TAKE ME AWAY. LIKE MS. KARP. SHE TOLD US TO KEEP IT A SECRET.

I THINK THEY'LL TRY TO HELP YOU. THEY WERE ALL REALLY WORRIED. I'M DOING THIS FOR YOU.

GET OUT.

IT'S MY DUTY TO PROTECT LISSA—EVEN IF IT RUINS OUR FRIENDSHIP.

IT'S ALREADY THE WEEKEND, AND I STILL HAVEN'T SPOKEN TO LISSA. WE HAD PLANNED ON GOING TO THE DANCE TONIGHT, BUT THAT'S NOT GOING TO HAPPEN.

ANYWAY, I'D RATHER STAY IN AND READ THESE OLD BOOKS I FOUND ABOUT ST. VLADIMIR. SOME WERE WRITTEN WHILE HE WAS STILL ALIVE, AND ONE IS BELIEVED TO BE HIS DIARY.

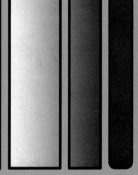

Today I healed the mother of Sava, but God has not allowed me to do such a thing lightly. I am weak and dizzy, and the madness is trying to leak into my head. I thank God every day for shadow-kissed Anna, for without her, I would surely not be able to endure.

SHADOW-KISSED. I REMEMBER NOW.

YOU'RE SHADOW-KISSED! YOU HAVE TO TAKE CARE OF HER!

THEY'RE COMING FOR ME.

THEY'LL COME FOR HER. YOU HAVE TO PROTECT LISSA. GET HER OUT OF HERE.

YOU MEAN THE ACADEMY?

LISSA. MS. KARP. VLADIMIR. WHAT AM I SUPPOSED TO DO?

THERE YOU ARE, PARTY GIRL.

I'M *NOT* GOING TO THE DANCE.

COME ON. IS IT BECAUSE YOU HAD A FIGHT WITH LISSA?

YOU GUYS ARE GOING TO MAKE UP SOON. NO REASON FOR YOU TO STAY HERE ALL NIGHT.

FINE.

HURRY UP AND GET DRESSED. YOU'RE NOT GOING LIKE THAT.

LISSA WILL BE AT THE DANCE. THAT'S WHERE I SHOULD BE.

MR. ASHFORD, MISS HATHAWAY. I'M SURPRISED YOU AREN'T ALREADY AT THE COMMONS.

YOU KNOW HOW IT IS WITH GIRLS.

DON'T WORRY ABOUT HER TONIGHT.

HARD NOT TO.

WORRYING MAKES YOU LOOK DEPRESSED. AND YOU'RE TOO HOT IN THAT DRESS TO LOOK DEPRESSED.

I'VE GOT TO GO.

...YOU AND YOUR SLUTTY FRIEND! I'M GOING TO TELL EVERYONE WHAT A PSYCHO YOU ARE AND HOW THEY HAD TO LOCK YOU IN THE CLINIC BECAUSE YOU'RE SO CRAZY.

HEY.

SLUTTY FRIEND HERE.

I'M REALLY NOT GOOD WITH IMPULSE CONTROL.

LISSA!

LISSA...

SOMEONE'S COMING FOR HER.

WHOOOSH!

STRIGOI?!

ROSE, I DON'T KNOW WHAT'S GOING ON, BUT YOU NEED TO GO BACK TO YOUR ROOM.

DON'T YOU THINK I'M PRETTY?

I THINK YOU'RE BEAUTIFUL. . . .

YOU ARE SO BEAUTIFUL IT HURTS ME SOMETIMES.

HIS KISS CONSUMES ME.

YOU GOT RID OF THAT DRESS FAST.

I'M FINALLY GOING TO DO IT.

CLVCK

GASP

I FEEL LIKE I'VE BEEN SLAPPED IN THE FACE.

WHAT . . . HAPPENED?

I DON'T KNOW.

UH . . . MY HEAD . . . L-LISSA? SOMETHING ABOUT . . . LISSA?

I HAVE TO TELL YOU SOMETHING ABOUT LISSA. BUT I . . . CAN'T REMEMBER. . . . I FEEL SO STRANGE.

I KNOW. THERE'S SOMETHING . . . SOMETHING HERE. . . .

HEY! THAT'S MINE!

GASP!

IT'S LIKE HE'S RIPPED PART OF ME AWAY.

UHN!

SHHNNAPPP

LISSA! SOMEONE ATTACKED LISSA!

SOMEONE CHARMED YOUR NECKLACE. GET DRESSED. WE'VE GOT TO HURRY.

HOW MANY STRIGOI WERE THERE?

THEY WEREN'T STRIGOI... THEY WERE GUARDIANS. NOT SCHOOL GUARDIANS.

WHY WON'T THEY HURRY?! I FEEL LISSA'S FEAR, FEEL HER MOVING FARTHER AND FARTHER AWAY.

ROSE IS RIGHT. THEY WERE GUARDIANS.

THAT'S IMPOSSIBLE.

YOU'RE SAYING THAT A GROUP OF PRIVATELY RETAINED GUARDIANS CAME IN AND KIDNAPPED HER?

YES. NOW HURRY, SHE'S GETTING FARTHER AWAY.

THEY WORK FOR VICTOR DASHKOV. THE GUARDIANS. THEY'RE HIS!

THEY'RE TURNING OFF EIGHTY-THREE. I CAN'T SEE THE ROAD NAME, BUT I'LL KNOW WHEN WE'RE CLOSE.

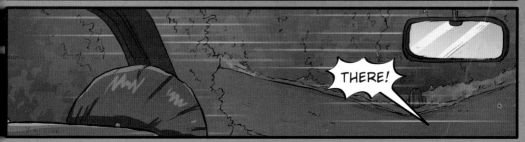

THERE!

LISSA, LISSA, WE'RE COMING!

STOP! LET ME GO!

COME, CHILD. I WON'T LET ANYONE HURT YOU.

UHN!

PLEASE CALM DOWN. IT WILL BE QUITE SOME TIME BEFORE THE OZERA BOY WAKES UP, AND I'VE ARRANGED TO KEEP ROSE OCCUPIED UNTIL AT LEAST TOMORROW.

WHY ARE YOU DOING THIS?

I NEED YOU TO HEAL ME.

FORGET IT! I WON'T HELP YOU!

SNAP!

GASP!

KRRZZZIIIIIIIZZZ

GASP!

BY THE TIME WE ARRIVE, THE VISION HAD FADED.
GOD ONLY KNOWS WHAT'S HAPPENING TO LISSA.

STAY IN
THE CAR!

THE HELL WITH THAT.

WHAT? WHAT DO
YOU SEE? WHAT'S
SHE DOING?

AH!

LISSA'S NOT AT
THE CABIN. SHE'S
ESCAPED INTO
THE WOODS. I CAN
FEEL IT. I'M GOING
TO KEEP HER
FROM GETTING
HERSELF KILLED.

WERE YOU BACK
THERE THE WHOLE
TIME?

AND YEAH, I KNOW.
YOU'RE GOING
WITH ME.

CHRISTIAN!

I CAN'T HEAL
HIM! I DON'T HAVE
ANY STRENGTH
LEFT.

SOB

HEY.

WE TOLD KIROVA ABOUT LISSA'S POWERS. SHE'S AGREED TO KEEP IT UNDER WRAPS.

GOOD. VICTOR'S UNDER 24-7 GUARD UNTIL HE CAN BE TRANSFERRED TO A PRISON.

I'VE HEARD ABOUT MOROI PRISONS. NOT ANYPLACE I'D WANT TO BE.

WHAT ABOUT NATALIE? WHAT HAPPENS TO HER?

HARD TO SAY. SHE CONSPIRED WITH HER FATHER... BUT SHE'S STILL A MINOR. WE'RE WAITING FOR A ROYAL COMMAND.

I CAN'T HELP IT, I FEEL BAD FOR HER. SHE'S SO AWKWARD... ANYONE COULD HAVE MANIPULATED HER.

DIMITRI... WHAT ABOUT US?

ROSE... WHAT HAPPENED BETWEEN US WAS WRONG. I'M AN ADULT. YOU'RE A CHILD.

THIS ISN'T THE CONVERSATION I'D IMAGINED.

BUT...

ROSE, IT ONLY HAPPENED BECAUSE OF THE SPELL. DO YOU UNDERSTAND?

EASIER IF HE'D JUST PUNCHED ME.

YEAH. UNDERSTOOD.

I HAVE NO REGRETS. THE MOROI ARE FALLING APART. STRIGOI PREY ON US CONSTANTLY. IN THE OLD DAYS WE WERE TRAINED TO USE MAGIC TO FIGHT ALONGSIDE OUR GUARDIANS. NOW WE'RE NOTHING BUT *VICTIMS*.

I AM GOING TO BRING ABOUT A REVOLUTION THE LIKES OF WHICH NEITHER MOROI NOR STRIGOI HAVE EVER SEEN!

FINALLY.

I HEAR WEIRD SOUNDS. GRUNTS AND THUMPS.

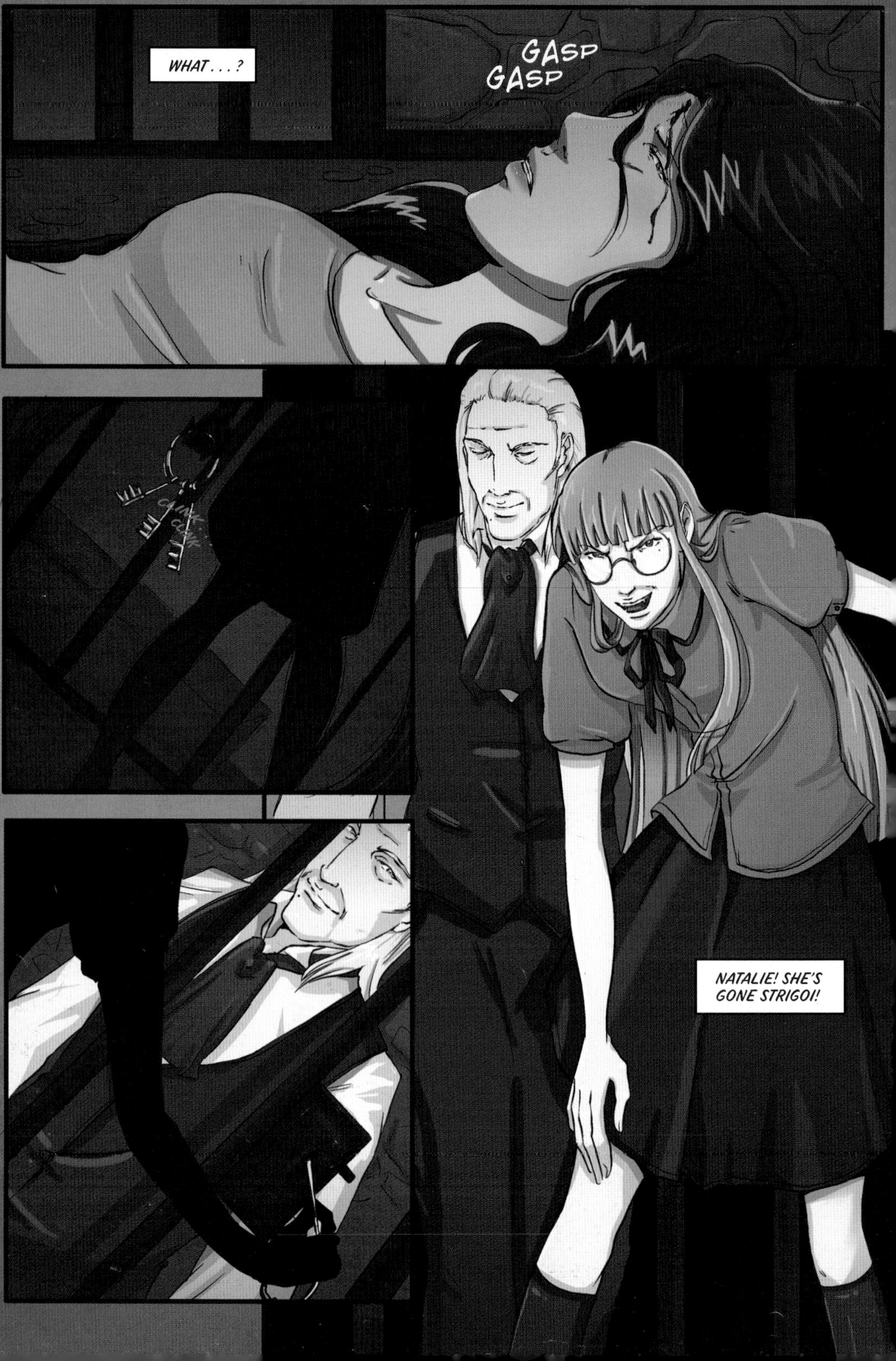
WHAT . . . ?
GASP
GASP
CLINK
CLINK
NATALIE! SHE'S GONE STRIGOI!

IN SPITE OF ALL THE TRAINING I'VE RECEIVED, I'VE NEVER SEEN A STRIGOI BEFORE.

GASP!

NATALIE... WHAT... ARE YOU DOING?

MY DEAR, TRY NOT TO KILL HER IF YOU DON'T HAVE TO. WE MIGHT BE ABLE TO USE HER LATER.

I CAN'T BELIEVE YOU! YOU GOT YOUR OWN DAUGHTER TO TURN STRIGOI!

A NECESSARY SACRIFICE. NATALIE UNDERSTANDS.

WHACK!

UHN!

MY FATHER'S A GREAT MAN.

VICTOR... VICTOR SAID THE SPELL... YOU HAD TO CARE ABOUT ME FOR IT TO WORK.

DID YOU? DID YOU WANT ME?

YES, I DID. I WISH WE COULD BE TOGETHER. BUT... ROSE, SOMEDAY WE WILL BOTH BE LISSA'S GUARDIANS.

WHEN THAT DAY COMES, IF A STRIGOI ATTACKS AND I LOVE YOU... I'LL THROW MYSELF IN FRONT OF YOU INSTEAD OF HER.

I... UNDERSTAND.

HUSH NOW. REST.

I'M GETTING PRETTY SICK OF BEING IN HERE.

HEY. HOW ARE YOU FEELING?

BETTER. A LITTLE GROGGY. DID YOU HEAL ME AGAIN?

YES. AND DON'T WORRY. THEY CAUGHT UNCLE VICTOR. HE DIDN'T GET VERY FAR.

NATALIE?

POOR NATALIE.

HER SACRIFICE WAS FOR NOTHING.

HE DOESN'T SEEM TO CARE AT ALL.

I SUPPOSE IN SOME WAYS THEY'RE PERFECT FOR EACH OTHER.

SO ARE YOU TWO AN ITEM NOW?

YES.

PEOPLE ARE GOING TO TALK.

LET THEM.

WE DON'T CARE.

—ABOUT CHRISTIAN AND LISSA? IT'S A PERFECT MATCH. BOTH OF THEM ARE FROM DISGRACED FAMILIES.

AMAZING. NOTHING KEEPS HER DOWN FOR LONG.

OH! MISS HATHAWAY, HOW GOOD TO SEE YOU. CAN I HELP YOU WITH SOMETHING?

YES.

I WANT TO KNOW MORE ABOUT ST. VLADIMIR. I WANT TO KNOW HOW HE DIED.

HE DIED PEACEFULLY OF OLD AGE.

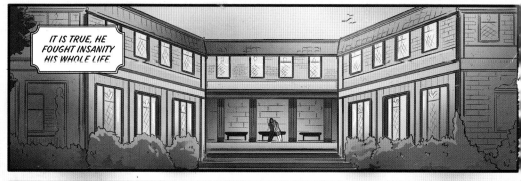

IT IS TRUE, HE FOUGHT INSANITY HIS WHOLE LIFE.

BUT HE OVERCAME IT . . .

. . . WITH THE HELP OF ANNA.

SHADOW-KISSED ANNA. HIS GUARDIAN.

END.